Poems for Edna

Heart To Heart
With
Ms. Millay

Poems for Edna

Heart To Heart
With
Ms. Millay

EDDIE MORALES

Copyright © 2014 Eddie Morales
All rights reserved.

ISBN: 1938094034
ISBN 13: 9781938094033

Table of Contents

To Your Treasonous Libido	1
Love is Everything	2
Lilacs, Poison, and Beauty	3
The Price We Pay	4
Mindful of You	5
The Gods Are Mute	6
Your Social Graces	7
Death to Bluebeard	8
Dear Jane	9
What is Meant to Be	10
I Hear You All Too Well	11
A Time for Innocence	12
Unblinking Eye	13
Self-Celebration	14
Columbine	15
In Love with Love	16

Beauty on the Run	17
Sorrow Blinders	18
Burning Star	19
Gaze Not Deeply	20
Obviously	21
To Diamonds and the Fiercest Blue	22
Complemented Beauty	23
On Stage	24
Of No Concern to Me Is Beauty	25
The Length of a Coffin Nail	26
Your Rationalizations	27
Stop Praying to Vanished Gods	28
Never Forget	29
Lesson Learned	30
History Rewritten	31
No Legal Recourse	32
Ageless in the Mind	33
Questions for Love	34
A Temple to my Love	35
Someday to Forgive	36
With Open Eyes	37
One Quarter Year	38
Two Against One	39

Supplication	40
Unfulfilled Dream	41
My Eyes upon You	42
The Master of Clay	43
The Countdown	44
Kingdoms at War	45
Scythe-Man Only One	46
Short Circuitous Dissipation	47
As You Wish	48
Rubbernecks	49
Until the End	50
Reflections	51
The Hungry Tomb	52
The Guiding Light	53
One True Heavenly Body	54
Ad Vitam	55
No Show Deities	56
On the Matter of the Poet	57
A Toss of the Coin	58
Poetic License	59
The Making of a Sonnet	60
Adieu Miss Edna	61
Titles of my poems and Millay's first lines	63

*This book is dedicated
to the Lady of my Tenth Muse*

A Note from the Author

The very first poem I read by Edna St. Vincent Millay, many years ago, was "I, Being Born a Woman and Distressed." I liked it. I decided I would read more of her poems and so I bought a copy of her book, "Renascence and Other Poems," then, "Millay: Poems (Everyman's Library Pocket Poets)," and then the whole collection, "Collected Poems."

The books sat on my bookshelf for several years, until I joined several poetry groups, and for one of the challenges, I was to write a poem in reply to another poet's poem. The very first poem in this book is the result of that challenge. However, it wasn't until at another poetry gathering, when I read both, Millay's poem first and then my reply, and someone commented they hadn't seen anyone do that before, that the idea came to me. I could write more replies to more of her poems.

Towards the end of February 2014, I challenged myself. Could I write sixty poems for Edna St. Vincent Millay from March 1, 2014 through April 30, 2014? That's sixty poems in sixty-one days. I wouldn't know if I didn't try, and so on March 1, 2014 I began to write my second poem in reply to another one of her poems. The poems here are presented in the exact order I wrote them. What I didn't expect was how involved I would get.

Once I started I couldn't stop. I went to bed thinking about the poems, I woke up thinking about the poems, and I would think about the poems at work, anxious to get home to continue my writing. No sooner did I finish writing one poem when I would start the next, oftentimes picking up the next morning where I had left off the night before, too sleepy to finish them the same night. If I didn't write for two or three days, I would write two or three poems on my days off.

On I went that way, until about six minutes before midnight April 30, 2014, when I finished poem number sixty-one. I had done it.

Upon completing the last poem, there came over me an overwhelming calm, a serenity so complete, I felt joy at the accomplishment, and was glad I had challenged myself to do it. I hope at least one person will feel the same way when they read these poems, and maybe Edna will like them reading them from the great beyond.

To Your Treasonous Libido

I'd say, no question, I'm the one possessed

By that one need which drives askew the mind,

And pleads a favor from your womankind,

No matter top, or bottom, or abreast.

For fair is fair, to feel a certain zest

By nature weathered, or by zeal inclined.

A pulse to impulse by your pulse you'll find

Is not possession but a course to best.

If by your blood you say you are betrayed,

Then all your efforts by your plans are laid.

Far better to concede to breast than brain,

For thinking's useless to the double cross;

And ever, after, should we meet again—

No words are necessary for your loss.

Love is Everything

Whatever sustenance I get from food

Or drink, or comfort I obtain against

The rain, or lifelines grasped to do me good,

And so on, none compare to love incensed

By its own need to give itself away,

Or be received without condition or

Restraint; yes, lack of this affective sway

May lead the bargain right to death's own door.

However, one by one, with love, I see

The saving grace that once may salvage all

Of what is life, and which I feel may be

The greatest, soothing comfort overall.

The flesh may eat and drink, stay well and dry,

But, without love, the soul is first to die.

Lilacs, Poison, and Beauty

The outer layer one presents may not

At all resemble lovely lilacs, yet,

What lies beneath may be exactly what

You seek—the beauty no one can reject.

Though, why it should be poisonous, I do

Not know; but, if like venom, drop by drop,

You drink, like Mithridates, of this brew,

You'll miss the burst that causes hearts to stop.

One may not have the face that turns a head,

But inner beauty is a powered mead

That's best consumed at once; and knocks you dead,

Yet lets you live the outcome of such need.

I'd let such beauty soak me through and through.

So, why not let it do the same for you?

The Price We Pay

Let Time himself forget to bring relief,

With fog upon my mind, if death is why

I find myself alone. For surely, I

Can only blame life's dark and cunning thief

For all my vivid memories and grief.

To have a loved one die begs one to die

As well, but even if I lived to cry—

I'd think—to honor love, though love was brief.

However, if betrayed by love, with time,

I fear, no countless years will ease the pain.

We are one tuning fork, yes, two in tine,

And cannot help but live in retrospect,

To think of love, though it drive one insane.

It is the price we pay to recollect.

Mindful of You

The sodden earth in spring has mind as well,

That favors you for having spent the time

Within her outstretched arms, her lakes that swell

With pride, her flowers that make the earth divine.

Her feeling's mutual in many ways.

So says the breeze that blows your hat aloft,

The moon that beamed you love, the sun's own rays,

Which tanned your cheeks, the skies so blue and soft.

The throats that sing all summer sing for you,

The seasons storm so you may notice them.

Remembered be your generations through

The years to come, and teach them well, so when

Your flesh becomes like earth itself, they'll give

There time as well, and know the hearts that live.

The Gods Are Mute

I guess I am your mortal enemy,

For life has always been my friend from birth.

Strange places are not curious to me,

And I cry often, but from greater mirth.

First breath is not within a babe's control,

But what ensues is prone to bit and rein,

Then steered, in later years, by one's own soul,

Along the paths that bring us joy and pain.

Address your worth and find the warmth you seek—

Your "self"—far more esteemed than any stone.

The gods may listen but they do not speak,

So let them kneel to right whatever wrong,

For you have all the power that is one,

And death will always come before too long.

Your Social Graces

I guess if opposites exist, then you
And I'd be converse in some love affair.
For I'd have no control of grief's ado,
Should, in some casual way, the papers blare
The news of your demise, and publicly,
I find myself the middle of that scene.
The world would know your love means all to me,
Right then and there, the likes no one has seen.
But if you must control yourself, to show
The world you know your social etiquette,
Then by all means, be graceful in the know,
That with my death, I'd be not to complain,
And you'll have face to save, like stone is set,
While underneath, you hide away your pain.

Death to Bluebeard

I will not to forsaken any vow,

Unwritten, written, otherwise—my word,

As gentleman; and well as one would know,

A lady's mystery, with time, is shared

At leisure's whim, or pulse, and only then,

By invitation. Trespass begged abuse

Your treasure, better left in private; when

One's greed betrays such love, one stands to lose.

Your friend, in greed, was of this thinking kind,

But know its spots the leopard has revealed.

It's best the knife in back than in the mind,

Where, over time, the flesh is better healed.

Far greater places now your heart you'll spend,

While his will only bleed out it in the end.

Dear Jane

If only I were now ten thousand miles

Away, your Dear John discourse may have hurt

Far less, and through the distance, my denials,

Like rotting fruit, the earth could turn to dirt;

But so it is, I'm not, and I'm to make,

You say, the best of what we have before

I'm gone, all used, no memory to take

With you, and by your leave, to seal my door.

The gentler side of nature you are not.

However, nature has contrived to boil

Our bloods, to biologic ends do what

We're meant to do, then swiftly move along.

We must comply, so not to nature foil,

Then say goodbye, forget, no pain prolong.

What is Meant to Be

Why bother with the ox-eye daisy game
Of love him or I love him not, and heed
What nature wants, and I will do the same,
Remembering the moments of our need.
Refrain from thinking why and if, and do
Instead, without remorse, and leave the rest
Outside your room; and even if not true,
Your love for me, I'll not complain, at best,
We had this time. And if it ends, farewell!
I'll know you loved the bitter-sweet, the smoke
Of autumn bush-wood, and the boding rain;
And in my mind, your notions will provoke
A smile, a note we did not love in vain.
You may find out you loved me all too well.

I Hear You All Too Well

How well you plead your case, with golden song,

To sing your heart out and be ever heard.

But who is listening? Before too long,

The world's asleep, as well the chirping bird.

Let pour such passion, as you speak, before

Ourselves, without articulation, give

Or take, and let your song upon me pour,

For I'll not sleep until we love and live.

As for the fruit on high, the greater height,

The greater bruise, and thusly, quickly rot.

Far better for the fruit to hang in sight,

Accessible to every passerby,

To eat right from the branch itself, and not

Keep passion hidden from the naked eye.

A Time for Innocence

So great is youth, their steps make tremble earth,

Like cherubs, though not so, to dance with song.

The spirits made are present from their birth

To ear, to heart, to say they all belong.

No matter silken threads or modest leaves

They wear upon their bodies unexplored,

Such innocence, in nature's bosom, breathes

The sweetest breath, with life its own reward.

Refrain from wishing them their end too soon,

For all too soon their time will also come,

As ours is swiftly, like a fading tune;

So let them jump until they're out of breath,

And let their strength and beauty overcome

The obstacles which have assured our deaths.

Unblinking Eye

If ugliness you see upon my face—

No spark to stir your heart, my eyes askew,

The valleys of my frown in deep disgrace—

Then truly love is of no use to you,

But must admit that even plainness knows

A beauty when to eye such beauty lands,

In mind innate, this nature's craft, which grows

Without control, still, heeds its own commands.

To love at mercy to its subtle ways

We are, (we do no less, we do no more,

We see no less, we see no more)—we do.

Imperfectly so perfectly obeys

A heart, which mind and eye cannot ignore,

No matter ugly or a beauty true.

Self-Celebration

I take my shouts and laughter for my own,

Where deities have nothing left to say,

Where on the banquet, on the altar thrown,

Our bodies spend the favors of our day.

We are the fruits, the trees, the earthen soil,

And launch ourselves, like moths, upon a flame,

Impatient, yes, before too ripe, we spoil,

To further bear the fruit which bears Love's name.

A woman and a man, so simply sweet,

A celebration of the joining of

Two selves, in complement, at last, complete,

Where nothing's left, and all is left of love.

We have the greater joy to shout and sing,

While gods are jealous of the love we bring.

Columbine

In patched and tattered dress, she plays her part,

Commedia dell'Arte tits-for-tats,

With ribbons tied to rainbows round her heart,

To suit the Calico and Cheshire cats.

So busily she works her magic strings,

To climb the moon, divert the stars, to kiss

The sun, and throw the switch to fancy things,

That please the master, if not gone amiss.

Her absence burns the changing pattern out;

In shadows, oh, the shadows dance about,

Where darkness to the one brings so much pain.

To lie alone, once love has fled, aghast,

You both were sure, I'm sure, it would not last;—

Tomorrow, she will play her part, again.

In Love with Love

To love itself, if you are only true,

Then equal are your thoughts to that of men.

Still, art of faithlessness belongs to you

As well, the better for it in the end.

I'll seek no vows, to hinder our embrace,

And make no vows, to change your nature's wit.

Fly after beauty, wildly love, then race

Away, and end all memories if it.

Perchance, someday, you'll change your changing mind,

Inclined, myself, to do the same, we'll see.

We'll make no promises to keep, in kind,

Pursue, before one's beauty flees, anon,

And we look back, damn promiscuity,

For we cannot undo what love's been done.

Beauty on the Run

Is handsome all that you desire of me?
Is beauty, of yourself, all you require?
You ask the rose turn never black, for we
Would fail, a vow destroyed, to douse our fire.
On this, the stage, you reconcile with flight,
Your moods so bound to change, and quick to run.
While I'm to love you dearly, all despite
The fact that Time so swiftly strikes—and done!
A year, I guess, with beauty swiftly moves,
With ugliness, the same year barely creeps;
And quickly as it comes, you flee, which proves
Your fickleness in bosom always keeps.
You'll hold me not too long, refuse my charms,
For sure, with time, I'll wither in your arms.

Sorrow Blinders

My heart, through sorrow, has put blinders on

My eyes, the pit too deep, yet filled with tears.

No mercy comes when joyousness is gone,

Instead, I wallow in my pain and fears.

No life is left then to pursue, it's all

In vain, or so I think, from where I've died.

Your kiss felt on my cheek, then I recall

The one who for my sorrow also cried.

So now, I'll celebrate the joy you bring,

Where all my sufferings will have to wait.

For fair is fair, as winter breaks to spring,

And you are still my summer's brightest light.

The fall will come too soon enough, and Fate,

I'm sure, will pause, you having healed my sight.

Burning Star

No numbered days a change in time would make

If even all your words in earnest flung.

I'd do to give, while you would do to take,

And in a moments heat, we'd both be stung.

It is a dream worth having, nonetheless,

No doubt, that we may have good days, and more,

And maybe nature's fruit may come and bless,

But in the end, all will be as before.

It ought be so if one's own nature true,

As lamb and lion, in the wild, are wild.

Your tenour is the best that you can do,

To do inversely would not take you far.

Take heed: no fracture may be reconciled,

If one can't touch, no matter close the star.

Gaze Not Deeply

Your life is far from narrow, nor consumed

By light, which, lack thereof, can't make you blind.

There are so many avenues to find

Which lead past woe, resist the death assumed,

Where if no heed, your best is surely doomed.

Do gaze on blinding beauty, if inclined,

But make it brief, for sake of your own mind,

Else wind up in your sorrow well entombed.

Refrain from gazing deeply to extreme,

Familiar things keep closest to your breast,

As well as any friends, though dull their gleam,

For they, ahead, will help you find a spark,

Where all will work out sooner for the best,

And find you see far better in the dark.

Obviously

You state the obvious, but I'll not be

Put out, for what you think is true, is true

For what you think—too perfectly of me,

While imperfection meets the same adieu.

This valediction is the nature of

It all, from nature's moment in a birth,

Until the moment none can stop with love,

For we are part of all that eats the earth.

Why dwell then on inevitable things?

If beauty here you find, then joy be found,

And fend not what the frosty fall may bring.

We seed the earth when time enough has passed,

So let not Time pass swiftly to the ground;

And kill your beauties, while your beauties last.

To Diamonds and the Fiercest Blue

No torture, have I, by design or not,

Inflicted so you dread the passing hours

Before me, and now threaten leaving what

Instead another would no doubt devour.

Such eyewash, reasoned out, is still a wash,

To where the diamond and the fiercest blue

Are asked to dull and cover up with ash,

Instead of burning to their tenor true.

My eyes will fire, with lightning if it crave,

For I am nature of a thing, akin

To flame; and I'll not hold you here as slave,

Nor suffer out your darkness at your whim.

I'll seek the peaks of Love, another's breath,

To prove to you, Love—has no name called Death.

Complemented Beauty

Perhaps we'll complement each other, you

In harvest of all beauty where it grows,

I harvesting it on the wind that blows

Your beauty towards a sky of clouded blue.

What suns may give to night, I'll look, and view

The moons of many faces, silver glows,

In phase, in contrast, ebbs and flows,

Where hate is always false, and love is true.

No creaking hinges ever frighten stars

Up high, where maybe your own eyes I'll find,

And with your downward gaze, I'll lift my own,

To find that single soul we may call ours,

And without fear, our hearts all intertwined,

We'll outgrow all the beauties ever grown.

On Stage

All you have said is one of Nine inspired,

Melpomene by name, who lost her song,

To tragic end, where seems you are attired

The same, and by your writings, tarried long.

Biology inveigled both of you,

Biography has opened up your eyes.

When next you write, make all your words ring true,

And weave no webs to capture love with lies.

The time will pass, your muteness purged from out

Your throat, where song may once more emanate,

And wonder not why you have loved, suffice

You did, if briefly of your own caprice,

Entreating friendship free of whim and doubt,

For where the curtain falls—comes fickle Fate.

Of No Concern to Me Is Beauty

If Beauty's massive sandal stepped on stone,

Then heard from far away, but never eyed,

And bare she walked, for Euclid's eyes alone,

Along his death, she might as well have died.

But never dread, we see no air but know

Its breath; no sun we see at night, but dream

It will return; though Beauty's bare, her glow

Is sound, in little beauties, all agleam.

To heroes give all welcome for their quests,

To mortals give what nature best can prove,

And on this earth, I'll find where beauty rests,

That I may touch, and hold, and see, and move

Before those souls, to see my gaze returned,

Who need no proof where Beauty is concerned.

The Length of a Coffin Nail

The fact that you now hold a cigarette,

Your piece of crumpet has been well devoured,

Where, up to me, the same, I'll soon forget,

And leave the Cheshire cat, by smile, empowered.

Though, even that, with time, you will dispel,

For in the total darkness shadows fade

Away, which "all" your lovers know as well,

The ones you can't recall, by will betrayed.

So finish now your cigarette, post haste,

For you must have a line in wait beyond

Your door, and so have little time to waste.

It may, one day, while looking in a pond,

Or glass, you see your face, and can't recall

If anyone remembers it at all.

Your Rationalizations

You never left your somber shores of youth,
Your ocean shanty always ready in
Your mind, that place you flee to for to soothe
Your heart, and so, you reasoned out therein.
If I were brittle seaweed cast from out
The sea, if "Sea of Love" the ocean name,
From out your door, a yard or two no doubt
I'd fall, where say you was the weed to blame.
My words were long, but short upon your ears,
My eyes were flames, but drenched in ocean brine,
My heart was bare, but pierced by all your fears,
My arms outstretched too short to make you mine.
You forfeited what love we had in hand
To be a stranger in the strangest land.

Stop Praying to Vanished Gods

The Cupid's arrow that you seek will not
Arrive from any gods of myth, but from
Some mortal's eyes alone, the crucial shot;
And rest assured, unknown, you will succumb.
You will not hear from gods who vanished long
Ago, much less feel any zing upon
Your heart, for in our time, they don't belong,
So all you wish for, in a blink, is gone.
Resist the search, while through some forest walk
You gambol, or, around some corner, when
Your thoughts seek other things, in idle talk,
You may just feel the sudden fusion then,
Where in some random countenance you fall,
And find, you needed not a god at all.

Never Forget

Oh, sweet Erato's lyre engulfs all who

Can feel the plucking of its heated strings,

Where from her fingers, mind inspired, ensue

The memories her love and lyrics bring.

This way, biology can never trade

For inspiration, for a higher love

Must override a lower love, obeyed

By every Muse who seeks her Art to prove.

Your soul should not be bartered with at ease,

Nor reminiscences be blotted out

By whimsicalities, to merely please

A lord, or otherwise, to break a bone.

When plucked the lyre, be free of any doubt,

And for your sake, be true to walk alone.

Lesson Learned

My dear, have you not learned and failed the test?
If so a traitor comes your way anew,
Such specter come from out the grave is best
Left in the tomb, for dead is past untrue.
But sweet your soul, this concept's hard to wield,
For you in quicksand take your faith to heart,
And craving dew, oasis breeze, you yield
To treason, love the same you saw depart.
Stop chasing colored phantoms, walk away;
Though not so simply done, I know, but still,
It is a matter of a stronger will,
Or you, yourself, you'll soon come to despise.
Though hot the sand, your sea must have its way,
No matter dark the night, your sun will rise.

History Rewritten

In every age, from kingdoms long since passed,

To Kingdom come, there was (there is and there

Will always be) a Garden Rose, surpassed

In beauty only by one angel fair.

So found his rose Odysseus two to none,

While Khayyam strolled within his garden great.

The centuries have seen their roses done,

When fall then fallen winter stood in wait,

And with his icy breath entombed the rose.

Were Lilith, Lesbia, and Lucrece unfair

To Helen's launching of a thousand ships,

Their fame would purely fade, restored by those

Of other summers, roses to declare

New kingdoms, each a name upon all lips.

No Legal Recourse

Like Guinevere, Isolde, I suppose,

Francesca too, when bound by earthly vow,

Or spirit vow, a friendship overflows

Past sensible domain, where weeds may grow

Abundantly, that if not weeded out,

May be concern for tragedies they spawn.

The flames the heart cannot resist, no doubt,

May sate by night, but take your life by dawn.

So which is it to be? True love or friend?

What potion may we take to quench our thirst,

Yet live the day? Carpe Diem! Not the end!

But think the matter forward, first things first.

They had, in ancient times, no legal course,

Where we should have the sense, and think divorce.

Ageless in the Mind

A cord, from birth, spans out until our death,
That navel string which Clotho's spindle weaves,
The length a measure Lachesis, from breath
To breath, will set for Atropos to cleave,
When some age suits her best, and there we stand.
One old in age? Agreed! No passion? No!
The soul has many for the withered hand—
The mind need only think the place to go—
With memories that cross the desert grains.
With music, conversation, poetry—
The lot! I'll take from life all that remains,
And crawl the land, and float across the sea,
But I'll not crumble in my mind, to wit,
I'll seek all passions till my cord is slit!

Questions for Love

What age was Love when first he felt his age

For love? What age can we agree is set

For love? The number Time may not engage?

What age between us should we say, forget?

In loves of May-December, is this best?

How does the heart determine whom to love?

Is there a numbered love where bosoms rest?

Besides, what can the numbers really prove?

Do kiss me now, and with each kiss instill

In me another number to my life,

That I may live a little longer, fill

More days with days of you, and when the strife

Of Time is near, be vigilant of Death

Past spring, should summer fall for winter's breath.

A Temple to my Love

If I should see, before a stone, such grief

Hard driven as it is with your distress,

So lucky would I count my happiness

With my own love, and I would grant relief,

By my own temple, hoping never brief,

To her, and spare her of such loneliness

You here describe, for one, to dispossess,

Will come in time, the one named tenant-thief!

My body be a temple to my love,

And I, the tenant of such temple, live

Beyond her expectations, thinking of

The times of worship both had then to give,

And if she die before I do, beware,

I will not live too long to linger there.

Someday to Forgive

No words of valediction will forgive

My words here spoken, lest you weep anew.

Said Shakespeare so, once more here to relive

The sorrow, sweet, though it is not to you.

So sad, that of the sweetest memories,

This sourest petal most you will recall,

Where being near is as if overseas,

And being close is never close at all.

Another sun will rise and clear the mist

I am; your flower, drooping, given time,

Renewed by greater moisture, petals kissed,

Will reach for sky, and I'll just slip away.

You do not see this, hindered by the clime,

And not forgiven now, you will one day.

With Open Eyes

One-sided love is only good for one,

Where should be hearts in one, but there is two.

It's always to the slave this love undone,

Confessed, or not, this much is doubly true.

If beauty in your agony you find,

Affections tossed, and you say this is just,

With open eyes you plunged, not blind,

Perhaps betrayed by nothing more than lust.

I query here: Who loves, and who loves not?

It seems, you both found something in the game.

So in the end, the score remains the same,

And off the stage, all soon should be forgot.

No matter what is here, no matter there,

To all and one, each heed your own affair.

One Quarter Year

May well-turned Summer be our gracious host,

This season best of all the yearly four,

Whose flame burns hottest, and endures the most,

And thus, to love, until to love no more.

Let's bring no weights, no cheerless, noble mood,

To spoil our only quarter of the year,

As long as signed your line, well understood,

The fall will take and race you far from here.

Wherefore, hear what I say to Summer: Burn!

But cook with slowest stir, and seething hot;

Delay our journey to cool-hearted Fall,

Where petal last be to forget-me-not.

If next, you say: Last summer's no concern.

I'll say: (I'll lie): I really can't recall.

Two Against One

What fervor Nature sews mankind come spring
The Reaper bids his cohort, Father Time,
By winter, to unravel everything,
And therein lies the nature of the crime.
These cronies flourish in decrepitude,
The dusk of day, the ebbing wave, the end,
The truest love-hate dissimilitude,
Where Nature hopes we save, they hope we spend.
They are the double-team to Nature's will,
The frigid wind and ice to summer's flame,
So pity, then, the blossom's winter chill,
And pity well the taming of desire,
And pity, yes, ourselves for love gone tame,
But vow, beyond, we start another fire.

Supplication

Now, barely fallen from my lips, I rue

My word already, and my oath, my head

Feels half to yours, that now I beg of you,

Play deaf; I here regress your word instead.

I deem you, love, an equal friend, in mind

As well, no sexist meaning here implied,

And I beseech, remit my joke unkind,

And give it meaning here instead, I lied.

However, should you choose, for I'm no fool,

A kiss would be the fairest makeup we

Can wear, if now my fault you overrule,

And with new words, a truer friend you see.

So, at your mercy, here I stand, alone;

I gave your word, please, give me back my own.

Unfulfilled Dream

You know that time can heal a wound is true,

But that all wounds can heal with time is lie.

The knife-cut flesh, with care, can scar like new,

But pierce the soul, the wound may never die.

Herein the problems lie, where love's concerned,

As well as beauty, ashes, Phoenix bare,

To think they will come back once they have burned,

Where truth then speaks, to most, the truth unfair.

Here so it is with dreams we've seen unsealed,

The one that matters most to soul than skin,

Though salve and dressing used, remains unhealed,

Where only burning memory will do.

However, this one thought, beware, is thin,

For once your dream is gone, then so are you.

My Eyes upon You

Though autumn has you barely in his sight,

My eyes see equal to the spring I knew.

The rose then close to summer's edge, the light,

The flame, the vibrant red, the one true you.

When leaves come fall, I'll follow in your spell,

And so, the vision that is you remains.

To all birds then gone south, let's wish them well,

Where I, with spring my own, your spring detains.

No less excited rose you'll be to me,

Though surely riper, like the fruit, your mind.

I'll too have ripened, lingered close behind,

So look at me, and eye to eye, agree:

Leave not declared yet Autumn has you beat,

Until your last red petal sighs defeat.

The Master of Clay

The hand that fashioned clay into oneself

Set you as well, so there's no need to praise

One more than Ozymandias claimed himself,

For bronze, well-torched, turns fluid in its blaze.

To cast a face, in effort to preserve

Whatever beautiful it is you say

It has, exaggerates what one deserves,

If even not to die, or death delay.

Consider one immortal in your mind,

If need you such, but keep one in your heart,

For you inside his own perhaps you'll find,

And as for death, we all must play our part,

For death, life, you, and all, are intertwined,

If true, one hand, is Master of this art.

The Countdown

My years have reached the old ahead of me,

Where I, October, see December's One,

And nothing's after thirty-one to see,

For in that midnight last, their years are gone.

I'll be in line then soon enough, my hack

Behind the hack in front of me, no tears

To shed, our suits the same, the last cold black,

Until my shiny, oblong box appears.

For now, I'll turn around, and backwards walk,

And I, with gold November, dance I will.

We'll sing and laugh, engage in idle talk,

And glad we'll be for never standing still.

Since I'm not one to sit around and wait,

You'll never hear me counting. (. . . Ten, Nine, Eight, . . .)

Kingdoms at War

You say a chamber holds a dying king,

His wounds most dire, no succor there at hand,

With moan he keeps within his throat, to sing

In darkness only, lest he lose command,

And this is what you see upon my face?

You see too much from nothing that you see!

My war is on, until I fall from grace,

The Grim One taking ever hold of me.

Until this Black Knight joust me to the quick,

I'll raise my voice, and sing him every pain,

And from the Gypster's book, use every trick,

Until the end, when face to face again,

He'll have to crack with force my aching bones,

If Reaper wants me six beneath a sea of stones!

Scythe-Man Only One

The harvester of souls no heeler needs,
No fledgling tenderfoot to ply his trade,
No Archer, Angel, Horse of any breed,
For there is only one, he swings a blade.
His chore is grim, this task of popping souls,
So lucky count your stars he did not show,
That Father Time held not the bell that tolls,
This two-in-one, who deals the final blow.
Enjoy your guest from heaven, bound to earth,
Immortal, if you think him so, to love,
With epistemic truth, the end of birth,
The balance kept, from harmony to strife,
Your youth was merely ill, could barely move,
He only "looked" like death! This saved his life.

Short Circuitous Dissipation

You might as well have worn a blindfold then,

Or patches on both eyes, perhaps, dark shades,

Or cataract affliction suffered, when

You can't call back your passion's escapades.

Or are your wraiths more likely spirit drink?

The ghosts that in the rain now tap and sigh?

This would explain the unremembered link,

The lips you kissed, and cannot scrape up why.

A lonely tree inspires no birds to sing,

Especially when fall has stripped its leaves,

When winter's mind has faded buds of spring,

And love, a leaf, looks at itself and grieves.

The winter's best for memories and all,

But what's the use of loves you can't recall?

As You Wish

Beware, if Time, acute of hearing, holds

You to your words, attends no less to age,

Of any sort, and what you ask unfolds,

Like nightmares in a storm, or seas in rage.

Time may shed skins you wear, remorse is one,

Where even shame, at length, is in decay,

But so might other skins, in time, made done,

If all in one, your skins are slipped away.

Your golden years too soon turn golden years,

No matter what the anguish Time has pressed,

What memories are skin, your joys, your fears,

No hurry should there be to final rest.

A crop of gray, a special chair, a cane,

Too soon will death be there to ease all pain.

Rubbernecks

A neighbor's nose and neck may be outdrawn,

A habit of the past, inherited

Perhaps, genetically, a kindred spawn,

And quite the rage with business of the bed.

So what, the moon, aglow, call out your name,

To like the cat, you seek to foul a bird,

Confuse the boys and girls, to spice the game,

But still, is no one's to be seen nor heard.

What's bought and paid is yours alone to keep;

So praise to Sex! Who loves you just as much!

It may be jealousy that makes them peek,

As if to noose their necks reach out to touch.

Well let them all be hanged, these fools outgrown,

Enjoy yourself, in nights not spent alone.

Until the End

Why, Father Time, covertly whittle us

Away as well within our private stage?

Suffice it not to you, invidious

Assailer, you've already cut with age?

Because biology's procession fades

Our youth, it proves not so with our desire.

From white to black, from crib to tomb, the shades

Of gray are many, as with carnal fire.

No matter lightless moon, or darkened sky,

One spark may be enough, no questions why,

Until the final day the stone engraved.

There is no keeping down a passion craved,

It's all a matter of the mind and will,

For death may be mistaken, lying still.

Reflections

If love is like a mirror, all you see
Is love; but if your love is like the side
Opposed, you will not see a love to be,
For your reflection will be then denied.
You might as well go blindly on your way,
With cane in hand, to tap, tap, tap the lane
Ahead, where gouged are both the eyes of day,
Than look to see you merely loved in vain.
Observe, yourself, be more the looking glass,
Where truth, your heart exposed, sends out your grace,
In time, a twin, your eyes all healed, and face
To face, onto each other's shine you pass,
For love reflects and is reflected much
The way two hearts, in love, reach out and touch.

The Hungry Tomb

My tomb will have to wait for me a spell!

Oh, yes! I vow, until I'm very old!

When winter's breath comes smacking briskly cold,

When I can't see Death's face, nor hear the bell

That peals my name, to heaven or to hell,

For I've got many days yet to unfold,

So many silver moons, and suns of gold,

Before I sink into some powdered well.

Then while its stomach growls, I'll have my fill,

I'll eat my life till not much left of me,

And eat until my body's almost nil,

Where skin and bones is all that's left to see.

I'll spit my last out then, and eye to eye,

To show my tomb, and Death, how best to die.

The Guiding Light

The Star of Ishtar seems to gleam within

Your eyes, delight, this morning-evening light,

This Venus, with her quarter moon, therein

The beautiful which makes the heavens bright.

This star you praise may feel for you as well.

From fervor in your words, your hearts align,

Your faces brighter burn an ardent spell,

Where each in silence feels the grand design.

When lost, so good to have a friend who knows

Your very soul, who makes your winding way

A straight pursuit, this guiding point that glows,

No matter far, great years, dark night, fair day.

Through desert sky, and every ocean tide,

Fair Venus and her moon hang side by side.

One True Heavenly Body

Where God and gods have failed, not so the Moon.

Religiously, the phases of his face

Adorn the sky, so oceans heave and swoon;

So lovers, under silver sheets, embrace;

So wicked and what ugly flee to hide;

So poets find the Muse which bars their sleep;

So one in sorrow needs no deity who lied;

And all of which this gracious orb will keep.

With visage full, the mightier will fall,

Or stand behind the brightest in our sky,

So through the mist, the orb and mortal eye

Come face to face, where no gods come at all.

We've seen no deity, since who knows when,

Where none have come, the moon will come again.

Ad Vitam

There's one, and only one, a single task

For Life: to give, and only give, one life.

No more, no less, and nothing more to ask.

Why some are born to bliss, and others strife,

Is left to Chance, who knows not heaven or

Of hell. All issues are in mortal hands,

Such joys as peace, such ills you find in war,

Where no such things a deity commands.

So be it then, what we ourselves direct,

These earthly thorns, or beauties of this realm;

Almighty, absent, ever his neglect,

The duty falls to man to take the helm.

Whatever then the path, one should head on,

For quickly as arrived, a life is gone.

No Show Deities

More heavenly are we than gods unseen,

From evanescent days, for we persist.

Reality has proved they've never been,

While we have certified we all exist.

We mortals soothe our pains through efforts of

Our own, where gods have never loved in kind,

Perhaps, because, although we crave such love,

All deities are phantoms of the mind.

No sun god ever climbed a sky of blue

For we have shown the earth's the one in spin

Around the sun; this tenet heresy

Was called, and to deny the gods a sin,

But they've not come to demonstrate them true,

So you'll not put to test a god for me.

On the Matter of the Poet

Are Three of Nine who cannot live alone,

The poet being vessel to each Muse.

Euterpe, grace to Lyric, being one,

Calliope, with her Heroic views,

And then, Erato, of the Love divine.

Which poet would you kill, in turn, to kill

The Muse? Would then be well the six of Nine?

This task is not as easy to fulfill

As one would think, each Muse a gift bestowed,

A symbiotic union, muse and man.

They walk together, heart to heart, the road

Of verse, according to the master plan.

So answered the debate—my own Muse cries:

"It matters if my poet lives or dies."

A Toss of the Coin

Pray tell, why give concern for worry's sake

When logic clearly states be troubled for

Good reason? One "faux pas" says only take

You mortal like the rest, and nothing more.

To be of honor is the labor of

The poet, whether it offend or bring

You fame, it flourish hate, or foster love,

And time will sort out every truthful sting.

Now, well you know your fears, so conquer them!

Write verses not unending, nor obscure,

And give them heart and soul, the pure to pure,

No matter they extol you or condemn.

When on the other side, you'll laugh a bit,

For mortals then must live the heads or tails of it.

Poetic License

My Poet of the past, appalling you
Would find this century of common verse,
This rhyme-less age, devoid of all you knew,
Where etiquette to ridicule is worse.
"Vers libre" imitates too closely prose,
While prose moves higher to poetic sense,
And intertwined, a problem there arose:
Which do we keep as poetry, without offense?
It seems to me, no rhymes have ever been
Confused, the good as well the bad, and so,
Confusing freedom we endure, as seen
By public works, to keep the status quo.
It's often so, I see it all the time,
Where they will surely prose who cannot rhyme.

The Making of a Sonnet

My Order is the Keeper of the Gate,

Of fourteen lines, which Chaos never breaks.

My mind, the Holder of the Key, must wait

With Providence, however long it takes

To out of Chaos give the proper word

Safe passage to my sonnet's inner field,

While out the gate, mad Chaos can be heard,

With enmity, to Order cry, "I yield."

And with the last of all my words in place,

There comes a silence, peaceful and sublime,

A unity of lines bestowed with grace,

The joining of all words in blissful rhyme.

No matter Chaos scream or jump about,

The couplet seals the gate, and keeps him out.

Adieu Miss Edna

If Pain was friend,

And friendlier his sting, with age,

He did so with intent to ease your

Journey through the portal,

There to bring your bones to rest,

And all your ills appease.

The more persistent Pain's pursuit,

Less grim the Reaper's scythe,

And like a split with you, a spat,

You've seen and heard the last of him,

Where then your enemy you did pursue.

You have the tranquil times,

Eternal tomb,

But then you argued with yourself to end.

Your life was his until the crack of doom,

For long you lived,

So also lived your friend.

Upon your death,

You live on evermore,

While so, at last,

Your pains have fled

Forevermore.

Titles of my poems and Millay's first lines

To Your Treasonous Libido
> I, Being Born a Woman and Distressed

Love is Everything
> Love Is Not All

Lilacs, Poison, and Beauty
> Thou art not lovelier than lilacs,—no,

The Price We Pay
> Time does not bring relief, you all have lied

Mindful of You
> Mindful of you the sodden earth in spring

The Gods are Mute
> Not in this chamber only at my birth

Your Social Graces

    If I should learn, in some casual way

Death to Bluebeard

    Bluebeard

Dear Jane

    I shall forget you presently, my dear

What is Meant to Be

    Loving you less than life, a little less

I hear You All Too Well

    Into the golden vessel of great song

A Time for Innocence

    How healthily their feet upon the floor

Unblinking Eye

    Love is not blind. I see with single eye

Self-Celebration

    Not with libations, but with shouts and laughter

Columbine

> The light comes back with Columbine; she brings

In Love with Love

> Oh, think not I am faithful to a vow!

Beauty on the Run

> I do but ask that you be always fair

Sorrow Blinders

> I pray you if you love me, bear my joy

Burning Star

> I think I should have loved you presently,

Gaze Not Deeply

> I too long have looked upon your face

Obviously

> And you as well must die, beloved dust,

To Diamonds and the Fiercest Blue

> I only know that every hour with you

Complemented Beauty

> Still will I harvest beauty where it grows

On Stage

> Sometimes when I am wearied suddenly

Of No Concern to Me is Beauty

> Euclid alone has looked on Beauty bare.

The Length of a Coffin Nail

> Only until this cigarette is ended,

Your Rationalizations

> I shall go back again to the bleak shore

Stop Praying to Vanished Gods

> Love, though for this you riddle me with love

Never Forget

> Cherish you then the hope I shall forget

Lesson Learned

> Once more into my arid days like dew,

History Rewritten
> No rose that in a garden ever grew

No Legal Recourse
> We talk of taxes, and I call you friend;

Ageless in the Mind
> Let you not say of me when I am old,

Questions for Love
> Oh, my beloved, have you thought of this

A Temple to my Love
> As to some lovely temple, tenantless

Someday to Forgive
> When you, that at this moment are to me

With Open Eyes
> That love at length should find me out and bring

One Quarter Year
> I know I am but summer to your heart,

Two Against One
> Pity me not because the light of day

Supplication
> Oh, oh, you will be sorry for that word!

Unfulfilled Dream
> Here is a wound that never will heal, I know,

My Eyes Upon You
> Say what you will, and scratch my heart to find

The Master of Clay
> What's this of death, from you who never will die?

The Countdown
> I see so clearly now my similar years

Kingdoms at War
> You say a chamber holds a dying king,

Short Circuitous Dissipation
> What lips my lips have kissed, and where, and why,

As You Wish

    Time, that renews the tissues of this frame

Rubbernecks

    I too beneath your moon, almighty Sex,

Until the End

    Now from a stout and more imperious day

Reflections

    When did I ever deny, though this was fleeting,

The Hungry Tomb

    Thou famished grave, I will not fill thee yet,

The Guiding Light

    Now that the west is washed of clouds and clear,

One True Heavenly Body

    Enormous moon, that rise behind these hills

Ad Vitam

    Life, were thy pains as are the pains of hell,

No Show Deities

    How innocent of me and my dark pain

On the Matter of the Poet

    To hold secure the province of Pure Art,—

A Toss of the Coin

    And if I die, because that part of me

Poetic License

    It is the fashion now to wave aside

The Making of a Sonnet

    I will put Chaos into fourteen lines

www.ingramcontent.com/pod-product-compliance
Lightning Source LLC
LaVergne TN
LVHW051849080426
835512LV00018B/3162